QUICK GUIDE TO FINANCIAL SKILLS

QUICK GUIDE TO LOANS AND CREDIT

by Marne Ventura

BrightPoint Press

San Diego, CA

an imprint of ReferencePoint Press, Inc.
Printed in the United States

For more information, contact:
BrightPoint Press
PO Box 27779
San Diego, CA 92198
www.BrightPointPress.com

LIBRARY OF CONGRESS CATALOGING-IN-PUBLICATION DATA

Names: Ventura, Marne, author.
Title: Quick guide to loans and credit / by Marne Ventura.
Description: San Diego, CA: BrightPoint Press, [2025] | Series: Quick guide to financial skills | Includes bibliographical references and index. | Audience: Grades 7-9
Identifiers: LCCN 2024013368 (print) | LCCN 2024013369 (eBook) | ISBN 9781678209100 (hardcover) | ISBN 9781678209117 (eBook)
Subjects: LCSH: Loans, Personal--Juvenile literature. | Consumer credit--Juvenile literature.
Classification: LCC HG3755.V464 2025 (print) | LCC HG3755 (eBook) | DDC 332.7/43--dc23/eng/20240405
LC record available at https://lccn.loc.gov/2024013368
LC eBook record available at https://lccn.loc.gov/2024013369

CONTENTS

AT A GLANCE

- People borrow money to pay for homes, cars, schooling, and other expenses.
- Banks, credit unions, and mortgage companies lend money. So do credit card companies. Lenders make a profit by charging fees and interest on loans.
- Credit bureaus collect data about consumers' loans and income. They use the data to create credit reports and credit scores.
- Lenders use credit reports and credit scores to decide whether to lend a person money and how much interest to charge.
- Making payments on time is the most important factor for keeping a high credit score.
- Many loans require a down payment.

- A secured loan is guaranteed with collateral such as a home or a car. Mortgages and auto loans are secured loans.

- An unsecured loan is made without collateral. It carries a higher interest rate. Personal, student, and payday loans are unsecured.

- Personal loans can be used for any large expense.

- Payday loans come with high interest and fees. They are risky and often trap borrowers in cycles of debt.

HANNAH'S FIRST CREDIT CARD

Last week, Hannah turned 18. Her older cousin Graham came to her birthday dinner.

"What will you do now that you're 18?" Graham asked.

"I don't know," Hannah replied. "Maybe vote in the next election?"

"You could always get a credit card."

Hannah made a face. "I don't think so. I've heard too many horror stories about

People must be 18 years old to apply for their own credit cards. But they can be added as an authorized user to an adult's account at a younger age.

18

interest and fees. I'll stick with my debit card, thanks."

"Using a debit card is a good way to learn financial responsibility. But it doesn't help you build credit," Graham explained. "Credit cards only charge interest if you don't pay off your balance. Set up

Debit cards pull money directly from a bank account. Credit cards need to be paid off later.

automatic payments. Don't spend more than you have in your account. Then it's basically the same as using your debit card, except you help your credit score!"

"What's the deal with a credit score, anyway? Isn't it bad to go into debt?" Hannah asked.

"Some financial experts say you shouldn't go into debt for any reason. That includes using credit cards. It also includes taking out loans to pay for college or your car or house," Graham said. "But those people are usually rich! They can afford to buy all those things in cash. The rest of us might need some help. And credit scores are important even if you aren't borrowing. My landlord checked mine before letting me move in. Just look into it, all right?

Your bank is a good place to start. They might offer a starter card."

OPENING A CARD

Hannah looked at her bank's credit card options online. She decided to talk to an expert about which would be best for her. Hannah made an appointment with Mr. Granger, one of the bankers.

"I want to get a credit card," Hannah told him. "My cousin said I should start building credit. But there are so many options! I don't know where to start."

"There are different kinds of credit cards," Mr. Granger explained. "And it's true that you can apply for one at 18. But there are some limits. Credit card companies used to take advantage of college students. A lot

Bankers can help people make decisions about their accounts.

of young people got into debt. In 2009, lawmakers passed a law to limit this. Now it's much harder for people under 21 to get credit cards. You'll need proof of income or a cosigner."

"What's a cosigner?" Hannah asked.

"That's an adult who agrees to take on responsibility for the credit," Mr. Granger said. "It's usually a family member or trusted mentor. The cosigner agrees to repay your loan if you can't."

Hannah frowned. Graham hadn't told her about all that. "I'm not sure my parents would be willing to cosign for me. And I only have a part-time job. Will that be enough?"

"Maybe," Mr. Granger said. "Some companies offer student cards. But your income might not qualify. A secured credit card will probably be best for you."

Hannah would need to deposit $200 to receive the card. Her credit limit would be $200. She could use the card for regular purchases. At the end of each month, she would get a bill. Paying it in full would build good credit. After a set period of good payments, the card could be upgraded to a regular card. Then her deposit would be returned. If Hannah didn't pay, the company would use her deposit to cover the balance.

Hannah liked this idea. It felt similar to her debit card. She wouldn't spend more money than she had. Hannah was glad Graham had talked to her. She was looking forward to building her credit score.

Using a secured credit card is a good way to start building credit.

CREDIT AND CREDIT SCORES

Credit is a person's ability to borrow money. With credit, people can have something before they pay for it completely. Lenders trust borrowers to repay them over time. When people qualify for an auto loan, **mortgage**, or personal loan, the bank is giving them credit. The borrower gets the car, the home, or the money up-front. Based on borrowers' income and history of

Credit cards and loans are forms of credit.

paying bills, lenders trust borrowers to repay the loan.

Credit cards are another way to borrow money. With a credit card, a buyer can receive goods or services without paying at the time of purchase. Credit card companies pay the merchant for the goods or services. They lend the cost of the purchase to the buyer.

INTEREST

Benjamin Franklin advised, "Remember that credit is money."[1] Borrowed money must be paid back later. And if a person can't pay it back in full, he will also pay interest. Interest is the price borrowers pay to get a loan. It is a percentage of the money borrowed. Almost all credit cards charge

COMPARING APRs

Credit Cards

Paying only the minimum required payment on a credit card can lead to huge interest payments. This chart shows approximately how long it takes to pay off different credit cards with a $500 balance when paying only the minimum.

	Card 1	Card 2	Card 3
Interest rate	17% APR	23% APR	30% APR
Minimum payment	$15	$15	$17.50
Time to pay off	47 months	54 months	67 months
Total interest paid	$198.36	$304.79	$510.95

Auto Loans

This chart shows different interest rates for a 5-year, $20,000 loan.

	Loan 1	Loan 2	Loan 3
Interest rate	5% APR	7% APR	10% APR
Monthly payment	$377.42	$396.02	$424.94
Total interest paid	$2,645.48	$3,761.44	$5,496.45

High interest rates mean higher costs for the same loan.

interest. But rates can vary. Some cards have an annual percentage rate (APR) as high as 36 percent. According to WalletHub, the average APR in 2023 was 22.9 percent. Interest adds up quickly. People can avoid

Some businesses offer loans with no interest, but people should always read the fine print before applying.

it by paying their credit card bills in full every month.

Most loans come with interest, too. Some loans have no interest. This is common at car dealerships. But 0 percent financing comes with risk. There are strict deadlines. If a person misses a payment, she may be responsible for interest on the entire purchase price. No-interest loans may also come with fees. The State of California Attorney General's website says, "Zero-interest financing and credit cards could be a good deal, but make sure you carefully read the contract, know all the hidden terms, and can promptly pay off the loan. Otherwise, you may end up paying much more than you think for zero-interest financing."[2]

CREDIT HISTORY AND SCORES

Credit bureaus create credit reports. To do this, they collect data about a person's credit history. A credit report lists personal information, such as a person's address and social security number. It also contains all of a person's credit accounts. Lenders report the type of account and when it was opened. They report the credit limit or loan amount and the balance. They also report a person's payment history. This includes late payments. A credit report also lists any hard credit inquiries. These show up when a person tries to open a new account. Finally, a credit report lists any debt that has been sent to **collection agencies**.

Credit bureaus provide a credit score based on a person's credit report. A credit score is a number between 300 and 850. A higher credit score is better than a low one. Credit scores are based on a few factors. The most important is payment history. Paying bills on time is the best way to increase a credit score. Credit scores also reflect a person's debt-to-credit ratio. This is how much money a person owes versus how much available credit he has. If the amount of debt is too close to the

Hard vs. Soft Credit Checks

When borrowers apply for loans, lenders check their credit scores. This is a hard credit check. People can also check their own scores. This is a soft check. Soft checks do not affect a person's score. But hard checks can lower credit scores. They can be a sign that a person is trying to borrow too much. One exception is rate shopping. If someone is looking for the best auto loan rate, she may apply for many loans at one time. These will all count as one check if she makes them in a short period.

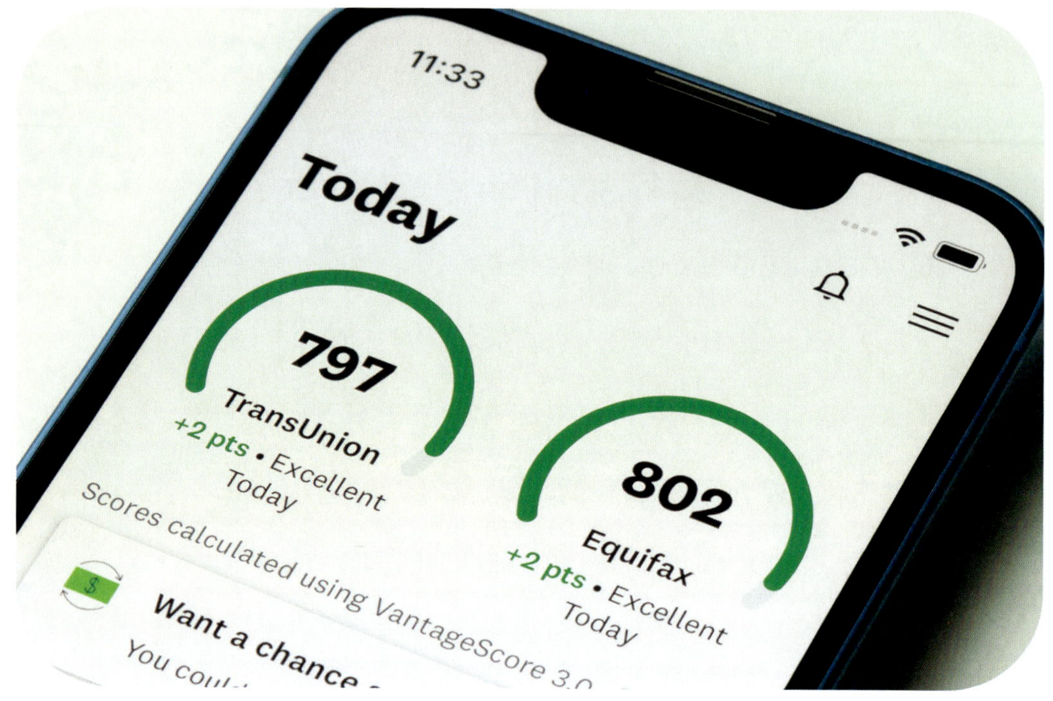

Credit scores often vary slightly between the different credit bureaus.

credit limit, the person will have a lower score. A person with a shorter history will have a lower score. Trying to open too many accounts in a short time also can lower a score. This is called new credit, and it signals risk to a lender. Credit mix refers to using different types of credit. For example, a mortgage, an auto loan, and a credit card are different types of credit. A person's credit mix shows a lender how well that person handles different accounts.

WHY CREDIT SCORES MATTER

Al Bingham is a credit expert and mortgage loan officer. He stresses the importance of having a high credit score. "The score [affects] practically everything: loan approval, interest rate, monthly mortgage insurance premiums . . . and ultimately their payment," he says.[3] When people apply to rent a house or apartment, the landlord usually checks their credit score. Landlords are more likely to rent to people with good credit. The same is true for insurance companies. They might charge more to insure the homes, cars, or properties of people with lower scores.

Landlords may look at a potential tenant's credit history to determine whether to accept the tenant.

Some employers will check a person's credit. Employers can't see an employee's credit score. But they can request a credit report. This is most common in jobs involving money. It can also happen for jobs that need security clearance. These jobs often work with top-secret information.

Good credit can open the door to more opportunities. A good credit score allows people to pay less to borrow money. People keep more of their earnings to use for other expenses.

CHAPTER TWO

CREDIT CARDS

A credit card is a revolving line of credit. A person borrows money by using the card. He pays the money back. Then he can use the card again.

People can get credit cards through their credit union or bank. There are also independent credit card companies. Many stores offer credit cards.

Many credit cards offer rewards. But interest rates and fees can cost more than the rewards in the long run.

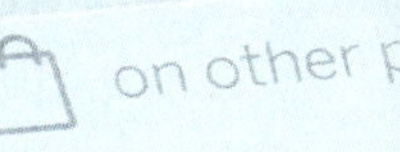
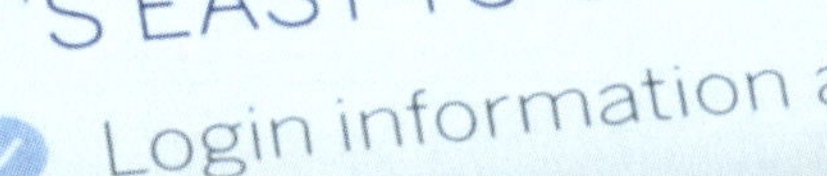

EARN $75 CASH BACK

after you spend $1,000 in eligible purchases on your new Card in your first 6 months of Card Membership. You will receive the $75 in the form of a statement credit.[2]

+

$0 INTRO ANNUAL FEE

for the first year, then $95.[3]

YOU'LL EARN:[1]

UPGRADE TO THE BLUE CASH PREFERRED® CA

6% Cash Back*	at U.S. supermarke up to $6,000 per y purchases (then 1
6% Cash Back*	on select U.S. str subscriptions
3% Cash Back*	at U.S. gas sta
3% Cash Back*	on Transit
1% Cash Back*	on other p

*Cash back is received in the form of Reward Dollars that can be redeem credit.

IT'S EASY TO UPGRADE:

- Login information and account history remain th
- No credit check

GET REWARDED FOR Y

WITH MORE CASH BACK[3] ON GROC

REWARD EVERY RECIPE

BE THE H OF MOV

6%

REWARDS AND FEES

Credit cards can offer rewards. Some provide **cash back** on purchases. Others give points. These can be exchanged for plane tickets and other goods. But some cards charge an annual fee. Cards also

Credit card companies charge fees to businesses that accept credit cards. To cover this cost, some businesses charge customers a credit card fee.

charge users interest on their purchases. If people spend more than they can afford to pay off, they'll end up spending even more in interest. Store credit cards often offer discounts. But they usually charge even higher interest rates.

Credit card companies make money through interest and fees. These include annual fees and late-payment fees. A cash advance allows users to get cash using their credit card. The fee is usually 2 to 5 percent of the money taken out. Some cards allow balance transfers. A person can transfer her balance from one credit card to another. People might do this to get a lower interest rate. Some cards don't charge a fee for this. But many charge between 3 and 5 percent of the balance transferred.

Anisha Sekar writes for the financial site NerdWallet. She says, "Opening a credit card should not be done on impulse. Review all the factors carefully before deciding whether or not it's worthwhile."[4] It's important for a person to understand all potential risks and fees before applying for any credit card.

BUY NOW, PAY LATER

Javier is in his first year of community college. He works at a coffee shop. He drives to work and class. One day his car breaks down. The repairs will cost $500. Javier has $500 in his checking account. But he needs that money to pay for gasoline, car insurance, and lunches during the month. His paycheck from the coffee shop is about $500. But he doesn't get paid until the end of the month.

Javier can't go without his car for a month. His parents had helped him get

Emergency Funds

Credit cards can be helpful in emergencies. But it is better to have an emergency fund. Ashlee Walton is an expert at an **investment** research company. She says, "It is literally just money that you set aside that you would have available in an emergency. If no other dollars are available, these funds could be used to pay for unexpected expenses such as car repairs or a hot water heater or to pay bills if you suddenly lost your job or had a medical emergency." Having an emergency fund will help save costs on credit card or loan interest.

Quoted in Aly J. Yale, "What Is an Emergency Fund?" Business Insider, *June 9, 2023. www.businessinsider.com.*

Inserting a card's chip or tapping for contactless payment are more secure than swiping a card's magnetic strip.

a credit card for emergencies. He decides to use the card to pay for the repair. That way he can drive to school and work. Money from his checking account will cover his other expenses.

The mechanic fixes Javier's car. Javier taps his card on the card reader.

His information is sent to the credit card company. Now Javier owes $500.

The credit card company sends Javier a statement. This shows all the purchases made with the card during that time. The total of all the charges is the balance. Javier only made the one purchase with his card, so his balance is $500.

MINIMUM PAYMENT, MAXIMUM COST

Javier's statement says he can pay a minimum payment of $20. It would be nice not to cough up his whole paycheck at once. But Javier's card charges 18.9 percent interest. If he only made the minimum payment each month, it would take 43 months to pay off. His total cost

Credit cards can come in handy to pay for emergencies. But interest payments can add up quickly if users aren't careful.

would be $686.59. Interest would cost him $186.59.

Javier does not want to spend nearly $200 extra. He makes a plan to pay off his card quickly. He asks to work extra hours at the coffee shop. Instead of buying lunch, he brings it from home. Javier can't use his entire paycheck on the repair. But because he spends less and earns more during the month, he is able to pay $400. He will still have to pay interest on the remaining $100 next month. But the interest will only be $18.90. Paying his balance early saves him money.

CHAPTER THREE

LOANS

When someone borrows money, this money is a loan. The person promises to pay it back within a certain amount of time. The lender might also charge interest.

People have been lending and borrowing for thousands of years. Banks, credit unions, and mortgage companies offer loans. Most people keep their money in a bank or credit union. The bank or credit

Loans can help people make large purchases, such as buying a car.

union uses this money to make more money. One way to do this is by giving loans. Mortgage companies give loans to people who are buying property. This includes homes or businesses.

DOWN PAYMENTS, INSTALLMENTS, AND COLLATERAL

Loans come with risk. For lenders, risk is the chance the loan will not be repaid. To reduce risk, most lenders ask for a down payment. This is money that the borrower pays at the start of the loan. Down payments reduce the risk to lenders. The down payment shows the lender that the borrower has money and is serious about repaying the loan. For the borrower,

Lenders may require first-time borrowers to have a cosigner. Banks often give lenders a better interest rate if a cosigner has enough income and a good credit score.

the down payment reduces the amount of the loan. This means the borrower pays less interest.

Secured loans are another way lenders reduce risk. These loans require collateral. This is property used to secure a loan. If a person fails to repay her loan, the bank will take her collateral.

BUYING A CAR

Shayla is looking to buy a car. She finds one that fits her needs. It costs $20,000. Shayla will need a loan. She goes to her credit union. The credit union requires a 10 percent down payment. This means Shayla must pay $2,000 up front. Now she owes $18,000.

Loans are usually paid back over a set period. The amount of the payment is

Loan Agreement

A loan agreement is a document. It lists the loan amount, the loan's purpose, the payment schedule, and the interest rate. The lender and the borrower both sign the agreement. It becomes a contract. This means both parties promise to follow the agreement's terms.

People taking out a car loan should carefully read the contract.

called an installment. For example, Shayla's car loan is $18,000 after the down payment. Her lender agrees to a five-year period for Shayla to repay the debt. This means she pays once a month for five years, which is 60 payments. The $18,000 divided over 60 months is $300 per month.

Loan payments are not the only cost of buying a car. People must also budget for insurance, repairs, fuel, and other costs.

Shayla does not have much credit history. Her credit score is only OK, so her interest rate is 10 percent. When the interest is added, the monthly payment goes from $300 to $382.45. This is $4,946.81 in interest over the five-year period. If Shayla can't repay the loan, the credit union will **repossess** her car. It will sell it to earn back its money.

CHAPTER FOUR

TYPES OF LOANS

Mortgages and auto loans are secured loans. But lenders also offer unsecured loans. These do not require collateral. They are riskier for lenders than secured loans. A lender gives an unsecured loan based on the borrower's income, credit history, and existing debt.

Personal loans are unsecured. People can get personal loans for many reasons. Someone might need help paying for a

There are many different types of loans.

Seller
Assignee

Many people use student loans to pay for college or other schooling.

wedding or vacation. Others use personal loans to cover emergency costs. A bank can't take these back to sell. There's no way to remake its money if the borrower doesn't pay. To make up for this risk, unsecured loans have higher interest rates than secured loans. They are for shorter periods of time, too.

Student loans are another unsecured loan. More than half of college students use federal student loans. They borrow money from the US government to pay for school. In 2023, the interest rate was between 5.5 and 8.05 percent. The Department of Education pays the interest on these loans while the student is in school. Once students graduate, they begin repaying the loans and interest. People can also get private student loans. These come from lenders such as banks, credit unions, or online companies.

Payday loans are short-term, high-cost loans. They are usually for $500 or less. A borrower shows a lender proof he has a paycheck coming. The lender makes the loan. Then the lender takes the money owed on the borrower's payday. Many people consider these loans **predatory**. Interest rates often range from 300 to 600 percent. Some companies allow borrowers to roll their unpaid debt into a new loan. High fees pile up. People get trapped in a cycle of debt. Alex Horowitz is an advocate for more affordable options for small loans. Horowitz said, "The average payday loan is $375, but the average

Some states have banned or limited payday loans.

borrower ends up having it out for five months of the year, which ends up costing them an average of $520 in fees on top of the $375 they originally borrowed."[5]

MORTGAGES AND AUTO LOANS

Buying a home is the largest purchase most people will make. Buying a car can be another major expense. Many people rely on mortgages and auto loans. These are secured loans. Collateral for a mortgage is a house. Homes usually go up in value over time. For an auto loan, collateral is the car. Cars usually go down in value over time. Because of this, the term on an auto loan is usually shorter than a mortgage. Most mortgage terms are 30 years. The longest car loans are usually 8 years. Shorter terms are more common. The interest rate on an auto loan is usually higher than on a mortgage.

Mortgage loans can have fixed or variable interest rates. A fixed interest rate

The amount approved for a mortgage may be more than a person can afford. People should look at their whole financial picture when setting a home-buying budget.

stays the same for the length of the loan. A variable rate can change. There's a chance the interest rate could go down. But there's also a risk it could go up. People with high credit scores get lower interest rates.

Mortgage loans usually require a down payment. But there are special loans that require low or even no down payments. These include loans for veterans or for some people moving to **rural** areas.

BUYING A HOME

Alex and Jordan Nelson are buying their first home. The seller is asking $300,000. The Nelsons visit their bank. They fill out a loan application. They report how much they earn at their jobs. They list their credit history. The Nelsons always make their credit card and student loan payments on time. They have been saving every month for a down payment.

A bank officer reviews the information. The loan's term is 30 years. The fixed interest rate is 7.94 percent. The monthly payment is $2,015. To qualify for the

Mortgage Insurance

Most mortgages require a 20 percent down payment. Some types of mortgages allow lower down payments. But they usually require mortgage insurance. Mortgage insurance protects the lender if the borrower can't repay the loan. It increases the cost of a loan. But it helps borrowers who might not otherwise qualify. People considering these loans should research mortgage insurance. It's important to understand the extra costs.

People must submit financial documents when applying for a mortgage.

mortgage, Jordan and Alex need a 20 percent down payment. That is $60,000. They need a credit score of at least 760. Their mortgage payment shouldn't be more than 25 percent of their **take-home pay**. So, their monthly pay needs to be about $8,060.

The Nelsons will pay $390,370 in interest over the 30-year life of the loan. If they had a lower credit score, they might have to agree to higher interest. A rate of 8.94 percent is only 1 percent higher. But they would pay $452,542 in interest over the life of the loan. That is $62,172 more! Having a high credit score will pay off over the life of their loan.

A loan for $300,000 is a lot of money. The Nelsons' credit history proves they are responsible borrowers. But the bank would lose a lot of money if something went wrong. Luckily for the bank, a mortgage is a secured loan. The house would belong to the bank if the Nelsons couldn't repay their loan. Then the bank could sell the house to earn back its money.

THE IMPORTANCE OF GOOD CREDIT

Understanding loans and credit is an important life skill. Jean Chatzky is an American finance expert. She says, "Debt certainly isn't always a bad thing. A mortgage can help you afford a home. Student loans can be a necessity in getting a good job. Both are investments worth making, and both come with fairly low interest rates."[6] Some loans are sensible. But people who use credit cards to buy things they can't afford may end up with debt they can't repay. Julie Higgins is a relationship manager at City National Bank. She says, "By making good credit decisions throughout their lives, children can save hundreds of thousands of dollars."[7]

A lender can begin the foreclosure process if mortgage payments are not made.

GLOSSARY

cash back

a rewards program where a small percentage of a purchase price is refunded; with 1 percent cash back, someone would earn $1 for every $100 spent

collection agencies

companies whose main purpose is to collect unpaid debt

investment

something purchased, such as real estate or gold, with the goal of earning more money than it cost

mortgage

a type of loan used to buy property, where the borrower pledges the property to secure the loan

predatory

designed to harm other people for personal gain

repossess

to take possession of something when a borrower can't pay for it

rural

having to do with the countryside

take-home pay

the amount of a paycheck after taxes and other fees have been removed

SOURCE NOTES

CHAPTER ONE: CREDIT AND CREDIT SCORES

1. Benjamin Franklin, *The Works of Benjamin Franklin Consisting of Essays, Humorous, Moral and Literary, with His Life, Written by Himself*. Chiswick: C. Whittingham, 1824, p. 163. *Google Books*, books.google.com.

2. "Zero Interest Financing," *Office of the Attorney General*, n.d. http://oag.ca.gov.

3. Quoted in Sarah O'Brien, "The Mortgage Rate You Get Depends Partly on Your Credit Score. Here's What to Expect," *CNBC*, February 25, 2023. www.cnbc.com.

CHAPTER TWO: CREDIT CARDS

4. Anisha Sekar, "Should You Open a Store Credit Card for the One-Time Discount?" *NerdWallet*, January 31, 2024. www.nerdwallet.com.

CHAPTER FOUR: TYPES OF LOANS

5. Quoted in Shelly Gigante, "The Dangers of Payday Loans," *MassMutual*, June 28, 2022. http://blog.massmutual.com.

6. Jean Chatzky with Arielle McGowen, "Debt-Tackling Strategies," *Oprah.com*, August 3, 2009. www.oprah.com.

7. Quoted in "5 Steps to Take Before Giving Your Child a Credit Card," *City National Bank*, n.d. www.cnb.com.

FOR FURTHER RESEARCH

BOOKS

Jennifer Boothroyd, *Managing Credit*. Minneapolis, MN: Bearport, 2023.

Tammy Gagne, *Credit Cards and Loans*. San Diego, CA: BrightPoint Press, 2020.

Kris Erickson Rowley, *Quick Guide to Saving and Investing*. San Diego, CA: BrightPoint Press, 2025.

INTERNET SOURCES

Anna Baluch, "What Is a No-Interest Loan?" *Experian*, February 7, 2020. www.experian.com.

"How to Build Credit as a Teenager," *Greenlight*, n.d. http://greenlight.com.

"Simple Loan Calculator," *Credit Karma*, n.d. www.creditkarma.com.

WEBSITES

Experian
www.experian.com

Experian is one of the three major credit bureaus in the United States. The Experian website allows users to check their credit score for free. It also has articles about credit, loans, credit cards, and more.

Money, Credit, and Debt
http://oag.ca.gov/consumers/money-credit-debt

The website for the Attorney General of California has articles on loans, debt, credit cards, common scams, and more.

NerdWallet
www.nerdwallet.com

NerdWallet is a financial education site, offering articles on various financial topics. It also publishes guides comparing different credit cards and loan offers.

INDEX

IMAGE CREDITS

Cover: © Backgroundy/Shutterstock Images
5: © Theethawat Bootmata/Shutterstock Images
7: © New Africa/Shutterstock Images
8: © Prostock-Studio/Shutterstock Images
11: © goodluz/Shutterstock Images
13: © Monkey Business Images/Shutterstock Images
15: © Hananeko_Studio/Shutterstock Images
17: © Red Line Editorial
18: © Steve Skjold/Shutterstock Images
22: © Tada Images/Shutterstock Images
24: © BearFotos/Shutterstock Images
27: © Deutschlandreform/Shutterstock Images
28: © DC Studio/Shutterstock Images
32: © Nattakorn_Maneerat/Shutterstock Images
34: © Trzykropy/Shutterstock Images
37: © LightField Studios/Shutterstock Images
39: © Wavebreak Media/Shutterstock Images
41: © Freeograph/Shutterstock Images
42: © lightpoet/Shutterstock Images
45: © Jirapong Manustrong/Shutterstock Images
46: © Ground Picture/Shutterstock Images
49: © dcwcreations/Shutterstock Images
51: © Fabio Balbi/Shutterstock Images
54: © tsyhun/Shutterstock Images
57: © Andy Dean Photography/Shutterstock Images

ABOUT THE AUTHOR

Marne Ventura is the author of more than one hundred books for young people. A former elementary teacher, she holds a Master's Degree in Reading and Language Development from the University of California. Ventura's nonfiction titles cover a wide range of topics, including finance, careers, STEM, arts and crafts, food and cooking, biographies, health, and survival. Ventura and her family live in California.